The Letters of Gratitude

Rob Martin and Jacq

Pollock

I am fortunate to be a resemblance, rather than a

replication of who I was yesterday

Jacq Pollock

Respect the past, and prepare for the future by

taking action in the present

Rob Martin

Contents

A Preface

The Letters of Gratitude is the culmination of our experiences trying to navigate our way into a new relationship, while working through some of what we would define as unresolved facets of our individual histories.

Where we were:

My recent past left me feeling empty and confused. In the last 2 years, I lost myself completely. I was a shell of my former self. The 20 year relationship, that had once excited me, fell peril to routine and lack of communication. Constant judging and expectations ran rampant. My self confidence was at an all time low, while my self doubt was at an all time high. **Rob**

The two years prior to this experience is probably best described as my most personally tumultuous and challenging. I had abruptly ended a negative relationship that I was in for 10 out of my 28 year existence. I found myself constantly redefining who I was. It was extraordinarily complex chipping away at the self that I had created within that relationship and uncovering the young girl who had entered into it. **Jacq**

Although, we can both recall it being the worst time possible to meet someone, we can both agree that we met for a reason. In actuality, we were both trying to find that place of peace and comfort within ourselves where we could heal some of the emotional charge that seemed to overwhelm the stories of our past. In the initial stages, our relationship was defined, as it often still is, by late night conversations that seamlessly meandered between recent past, the historicism of our lives, and our aspirations for the future. It was during these late night conversations that we lightly grazed on old wounds: pains that were forgotten or never actualized in expression. Writing *The Letters of Gratitude* began as an individual experience for us: we wanted to utilize the written word to heal, uncover, discover and celebrate our unique stories and life experiences. We both truly wanted to move forward in this world with the same excitement, exhilaration and passion that overwhelms the youth of this world.

In a somewhat ironic twist, the seemingly simple and straightforward writing program we developed for ourselves, turned out to be one of the most rewarding and challenging experiences of our lives.

The core concept was to write 30 letters to ourselves defining and exploring our past under the title of a list of 30 words that we had selected. Central to our thinking was the decision to write in a way that we were able to arrive at a place of gratitude. We have all had experiences in our lives that we could characterize as colorful, and our natural reaction is overwhelmingly "get over it and move on" or "time heals all wounds". Truth be told, this had not worked for either of us and this became quickly apparent during our 30 day writing process. The 30 days of writing was continual head on collision with self. We rode the wave of emotional pain and euphoria of honesty throughout the month. In all honestly, we were not entirely sure we would emerge from this writing process united.

Although we always intended to share our writing with one another, it was never meant to bridge our lives, or enhance our communication with one another; but it did. We both literally laid ourselves on the table: 30 *Letters* that encapsulated our thinking and our past. No hiding, no selective stories, and no emotional guards: perhaps the most vulnerable we have ever been in our lives; we sat before each other *Letters* in hand. Sharing the *Letters* was like sitting naked before a stranger gazing intently upon you. It was an incredibly vulnerable position to be in, but indescribably empowering. Beneath it all, this is who I am. Take it, or leave it. Together we shared innumerable tears and whole hearted laughs. In the end, we shared our selves entirely.

Without question, this experience has brought us back to who we truly are at the core of ourselves. We know who we were and were not going back. Today, we both stand as individuals proud of our past and certain of who we are. As a couple, it has ultimately defined the way that we communicate with each other. We have a love for each other that is firmly rooted in our individual happiness and authenticity. Truly, we love each other as is---no touching up required.

What began as our individual journey is one that we both felt the intent need to share. This writing process profoundly altered us both as individuals, and united us in such an incredible way that it seemed implausible to keep as our own unique experience. We are both motivated to share this because we know how life altering this was for us and we both hold firm to the belief that it will be for others.

The Letters of Gratitude begins with our experience, but will only truly begin with yours.

From our Journey to Yours---Rob Martin and Jacq Pollock

Prologue

The *Letters of Gratitude* is a journey of healing and inspiring the soul through the written word. This writing process is a true celebration of self and rewards your individual truths by scribing your unique story of becoming. The challenge of expediting the past requires that we take a long and reflective gaze back to the paths that we have walked. Deciphering the past through language has the power to reveal who we are, how we see the world, and how we got there. Linguistic unraveling of self reveals where we stand in our lives, which is not necessarily somewhere that we desire to be. In order to achieve the peaceful presence we all seek, we also must project our ideals on the future through the written word. Peacefully and lovingly accepting who we are today requires honestly looking at our past, and having the courage to scrutinize and re-evaluate the diction of our lives.

We all see the world in accordance to our individual experiences, thoughts and emotions: this manifests itself through language. All too often, life occurs and we mechanically progress forward without reflection; we are continually shifting as individuals as we navigate ourselves through the world. Our ideas change as they are challenged, but we rarely take the time to posture this. Essentially, when we do not recognize our individual evolution, we become in danger of not recognizing self: who we have become. The *Letters* are a life altering tool that beckons and challenges to you to be vulnerable and honest with yourself, and connect with you have become.

The Letters of Gratitude is an intensive writing process that invites you dedicate 30 days to your personal history and scribe the most influential

aspects of your psyche and pivotal monuments of

your life. Through the scope of gratitude and 30

words you have the opportunity write a *Letter* to

your present self: how you define the word, how it

shapes the way you see the world, and the

experiences that have shaped your discourse. When

you are honest with yourself, you will find buried

beneath the individual you thought stood before

you, a complex story of wounds forgotten,

experiences discarded, inspirations unspoken, and

ideas unformulated. The 30 *Letters* are a snapshot

of your past and your thinking; they are able to truly

capture what makes you individually and uniquely

you. Writing through the scope of gratitude is

essential and has an extraordinary twofold effect:

we become grateful for all that encapsulates our

past, and we begin to see everything we encounter as having a positive influence in shaping our life.

To ensure this optimistic and idealistic scope continues forward we must close the chapters of the past by surrendering to the present and letting go of what has gone before. After writing our current stature of the 30 words, we also challenge you to create 30 brief optimistic statements for your future. Scribing your new vision for what you want to achieve in your future has an remarkable effect. When you project idealism ahead of where you walk, it is empowering and inspiring when you stumble upon it. The world truly manifests what words you put forth.

30 days of writing through words and gratitude creates 30 intense vignettes of who you are, and

how you came to be. Writing has the uncanny ability to uncover wounds that have been deep seeded within in your heart and soul. When we deeply explore self we discover scars lost and our pains of the past become fully exposed. We must reveal and release in order to heal. This process is not for the faint hearted and is a journey that takes full commitment and courage. In the end, the rewards are copious if you are honest to yourself.

Words:

The pages that follow are not only words. Rather, they are a powerful series of letters consciously strung and sewn together by two very different minds that have embodied two entirely different worlds. Worlds polarized by gender, age and life experiences. The collision of these lives has ultimately created the language and movement of

gratitude that follows; the essence of which was

ignited in a moment, composed within 30 days and

boundlessly carries forward. Undeniably, the roads

they walk and the people they encounter will see

and feel the impact of both the admiration, and the

saturating effect gratitude plays in their lives. Both

have looked back, deep within themselves and

project on their future a world ingrained in

gratitude.

Gratitude is a powerful lens which, if we gaze

through thoughtfully, we can come to a place where

we are better able to understand ourselves. Unlike

the tradition posture of pausing, reflecting and

releasing: this process ensures you also capture,

share and look through a scope of optimism. When

we take on the challenge of exchanging our view of

life for a new meta-cognitive process that is deeply rooted in the essence of positivity, a tremendous shift occurs. By making this conscious decision to look deep within ourselves, including everything that embodies us, and recording it, we can get to a place of peace, where we are truly able to surrender to the world around us. A space not only firmly, but also thoughtfully and thankfully grounded between our past and what lies ahead. This process combines both writing and thinking carefully about words, and from this you will be able to see and live more clearly. In the end, you will create and have a new language to live by.

This is a journey deep within the psyche of self that has enabled us to see and better understand the roads we have travelled. To truly see how we came to be; who we are today, and what roads lie ahead.

 A triumphant challenge, but a journey everyone should embark upon.

Inside these pages you will see uncensored, raw and honest writings of two people who came together in the search of a way to better their lives and had the courage to write *Letters* to self. They were able to discuss some of their deepest secrets and rid the masks so comfortably worn by many. It is an adventure that shifted their lives for ever and through their learning and growth they felt the need to share their experience with others. Initially, it may appear to be a simple writing exploration; but authenticity and honesty has its difficulties. Throughout the process mental and emotional shifts occur, as they did with Jacq and Rob, as they progressed through the process. Two very different experiences, but ultimately led them to the same outcome: the dissolution of fear has created a

freedom within, a greater sense of self worth, and

individual empowerment.

The Inspiration

Deep within us there are roads that we meander and travel in our minds. While we are physically present in our world, we travel within our mind to places that remain unknown to the world around us. Whether we have ideas that we opt to keep within, pride that we choose to not celebrate, or pain we simply chose to not burden another with. Ultimately, we choose not to share what is within us because it easier to internally converse. Within our minds, we have a world that we keep for ourselves. It is within this world that we have moments of energy and enthusiasm for that which lies ahead. Too often, these emotions are forgotten and we progress forward without listening to what we believe to be right. The reality is that life occurs and we ignore that voice within us. When we listen to what presides within us, a remarkable voice speaks. The real magic occurs

when we listen.

Here are our unique inspirations for the Letters---

this is how it all began.

Rob

A weekend away: an escape. It was a chance to be with Jacq and to really have her to myself: free of all outside influences; work, roommates, friends, everyday life. A chance to explore and just be! The setting: a remote island, a quaint cottage, a hot tub ... awesome. Met by friendly strangers, the laughs and loud music began. We had spent a lot of time alone together but this was different. I felt free! Good food and drinks accompanied by flawless company: the recipe was perfect. I remember thinking that this is how life should be; enjoying every moment of every day, without a worry in the world.

The day turned to night. We came together completely. Out of nowhere the words rang loud and clear.

"Letters of Gratitude: page by page we weave the
worlds."

My heart raced. I recall after the first week that we
had met that, we would do something together. Our
views on life and people although expressed very
differently ran along the same lines. Many times the
same thing was said but just in different tongues. I
knew the words *Letters of Gratitude* that came out
of her mouth felt right. I had no idea of what the
journey we were soon to embark on would be, but,
it didn't matter. I just instantly believed that this
was it! What I did know as the conversation
progressed, whatever it was to be we had to grow. I
was ready to change to change my life. This was
really an opportunity to take a good look at myself,
my past and learn from those experiences rather

than keep certain events hidden: buried deep within my soul where they would have stayed until my body hit the dirt. This was my chance to cleanse myself and break free. This really was the perfect opportunity to honestly look at myself and I welcomed this.

Excited by these words we spoke till dawn. Wine and beer turned into pots of coffee as we shared and weaved our ideas together. The conversations continued daily and as time moved forward so did the scope of what lay before us. Everything just seemed to fit. It was so natural. We soon realized what a powerful process could potentially possess for us. We laughed uncomfortably as we both agreed that writing the Letters could do one of two things for us: bring us together, or destroy us. We both acknowledged that either way that we personally would be better for it, and committed to

taking this journey.

Gratitude naturally fell into place and the journey

began ......

Jacq

In a dark room, a world away from the challenges

our lives had life in their wake, passion eroded into

a series of events that neither of us expected. The

room was energized with inspiration---so much so

that a carefully scripted list of sexual endeavors

would soon take a fall to the sudden urgency of the

moment. He uttered words that I would soon forget,

yet the essence of the emotional aurora, in that

space, at that time would not. It seemed to come

out of no where---the words, the thoughts, and the

undeniable energy. It struck us both with a great

force. In moments like this, there are truly only 2

choices: be moved, or move away. Words

exchanged at a pace that was quickened by an

inescapable synergy; a collision of forces: of lives

lived, of moments lost, of challenges yet to have

been met, tears yet to have been shed, smiles yet to

have had, laughter yet to be known.

"Letters of Gratitude: Page by page, we weave the worlds"

"That is it!"

Burned into the psyche. Smoldered deep within a place, energized into the minds that were meant to be occupied; minds that were meant to be slipping into a space defying cognition. No thinking---a supposed escape from the painfully encroaching surrounding worlds, relations and complications that we so often define as the monotonous stress of real life.

Regardless of what was before, or what lay ahead--- the moment had been defined and was irrevocably clear---this is it. Unfolding, un-creasing wrinkled linens left to be pressed. What if. What if the course of what was to follow would be left to the belief of this moment. Two people, two lives, two choices and a new lens to look through: Gratitude.

From the moment that we had met, one thing was clear: conventions would not dictate the course. Invites normally rejected, opportunities for possible engagements normally unfulfilled, pick up lines normally passed, the offer of a ride home to a stranger rarely spoken, a ride home never taken, an offer of tea for the first time uttered, and the acceptance simply because the moment had arose. Collision.

In the months that would follow, we were inseparable. Opposite work schedules, separate homes, complicated families, polar circles of friends---for every excuse to not make a phone call, to not accept an invitation, to claim our lives lived were far too complicated---for every excuse to evade, to run, we chose not to. Instead, we clung to each other. Unlike every other relationship I have ever been in, there was comfort, solace in knowing, believing that people meet for a reason. Belief that there was something to be gained, learned from this encounter; a lesson perhaps. No television, hours of conversation slipped away into days, months. An eclectic montage of music rythmatically eavesdropped on these lives that were meant to be busily living elsewhere. Together, we picked up our pens and scribed the road that took us to where we were. Together we wrote.

The Journey

While we both endured and committed to the same process, we had two very unique writing experiences. For each one of you who embarks on this challenge, your journey will be as individual as you are. Here is our journey of us and how we got here:

ROB

I knew that this would be an experience that could push me, pull me, essentially throw me around but deep inside I really felt I needed to get some clarity of self. I felt ripped in two! I had met this incredible woman who sparked my soul at a time of such devastation. I had left a long term relationship and my daughter's emotions were still raw. I was so confused! I knew what I wanted. I wanted happiness in my life and for all of those around me, but felt lost. I knew that writing *The Letters of Gratitude* was right. Secretly, I feared that by exposing myself fully to a woman that I had known for such a short time would be detrimental to our relationship. I shared that I felt this would bring us together in a way that I did not know existed, or it would destroy us. She looked into my eyes and said "let's do this!" The excitement that built from this with my partner really ignited a fire within: something that opened my eyes. With nothing more in mind than the potential for self growth and capturing peace and happiness in my life, we sat and shared the potential of this.

The concept naturally fell into place. This started as an individual journey: both writing freely and from the heart, sharing experiences and thoughts on our pre-selected words through thoughts of gratitude. We compiled 30 words that would encapsulate the essence of a rounded experience.30 words in 30 days. Commit to it! Live it! Learn from it! Feel it! Free it! Grow! I remember my energy starting - I was super-charged and ready to make the necessary shift that would catapult me into a new realm of possibilities. Easy, a word a day, not a problem: how hard could this be?

The mind is very interesting because once pen hits parchment, you dive within yourself. You commit to those words. They represent you! This isn't just a writing exercise, it's a living exercise. This is where the real work begins. When you are grateful for the lessons in your life, you begin to want something different. I needed to break habits: deep seeded reactions that allowed me to respond naturally through emotions of hope, fear, anger, passion and so on. Truthfully, "if you do what you've always done, you get what you've always got." I started looking at the words. What do they look like to me? What do they represent? For me it was important to sit and focus on the word. Sometimes the ink flowed freely from the pen, and other times it was more challenging. You have to remember that there are many ways that most words can be spun. They can be linked to more than one story, so I continually asked myself "where does this word want to take me?" That's when things started happening for me. I started looking back. Not just over the last couple of years but way back. I started seeing demons that had obviously been hiding for a long time: the physical and emotional reprimand from men and women, drugs, alcohol, violence, abuse, death, pain, fear, tears flowed down my cheeks as my mind started opening up to myself. These were pieces of me. This is when I realized that you need to be awake; it is time to be honest. Stories kept popping up for me; I would stop and acknowledge them.

I found there were days that I would fall deep within myself. Jacq always gave me my space and never questioned where I was at and I did the same for her. As a result of this process, I realized that when someone is quiet and not talking that it has nothing to do with me. Normally, when I saw someone in pain I would jump into my Superman suit and want to fix everything and make everything better. This was not my place to do that. Everyone is responsible for their own feelings and emotions as I am for mine. I really started feeling a shift as we moved through this process. It's tough. I am not going to pretend its not. Diving deep within, took a lot of courage. To uncover skeletons and acknowledge those experiences as being real and to be able to look at what I have learnt from that experience is challenging. How can you learn anything from watching your brother jump in front of your mother's boyfriend and antagonize him to distract him so I wouldn't cop a beating? What could I learn from a tutor verbally and physically abusing me at my boarding school at 10 years of age? Is it possible to learn anything from having an Uncle put a knife to your throat and threaten to slice you into little pieces? What could I possibly learn from having an Aunty smash a frying pan over my head because I didn't do the dishes straight away? Although these are a few realities in my world that I didn't write about, they still came forward and I was able to acknowledge them because this process opened the doors to my past. To be able to look for lessons learnt and to look at the experience through a lens of gratitude shifts the experience. I am grateful for my brother and his devotion to me even though our relationship has been somewhat distant over the last year. I am grateful for being able to reconnect with that tutor many years later and let him know that what he did was wrong and that I felt sorry for him! I am truly grateful for being able to contact my Uncle while doing my letters and tell him that I forgive him! I am grateful for understanding now why I don't like doing the dishes!!! :)

The journey that awaits you holds such rewards, but it cannot be taken lightly. This is quite possibly one of the biggest commitments that you can make to yourself. It was for me. If you are true to yourself your heart opens and creates such huge possibilities for your life. Am I fixed? Am I issue free? Not even close, but I am growing and learning everyday and have such appreciation for the Journey you are about to embark on. It has changed my life and wish the same for you.

Jacq

30 days: lost within the psyche of self. Diving deep into the dark depths of my short, what I had previously defined as an uncomplicated and extraordinarily fortunate existence. I would have readily characterized my personal history as relatively straightforward: stumbles reconciled with strong stances, continually progressing forward: oddly, a typical life.

When Rob stated that this process would either bring an end to our relationship, or bring us closer together I half chuckled. *If he only knew me.* He had known me for a mere few months, thinking and writing were not in any sense of the word new for me. The concept of reflection has always been intricately connected to my existence. I thought I had always been in a state of constant awareness of self. Analyzing, reimaging, and rewriting my past;

a quasi-practice run, just in case I were to encounter

it all over again, I would be prepared. As for words,

they were my playground. My safe haven;

language has always been a symbolic manifestation

of my mind that somehow found fruition on paper.

As a little girl, I can recall turning to blank pages,

grappling a pen as a means for resolving life's

mishaps, or someone to share in my joy, or the

farfetched concoctions that I had imagined. *If he*

only knew me.

When we started the writing process I must admit

my amusement with the actuality of writing with

someone. The notion of experiencing such intimacy

was a wondrous cocktail of fear and excitement.

Something I had yet to taste. Prior to this, writing

had always been a very intimate and private activity

that I reserved for those solemn nights where interruption was an impossibility. In reality, it was rarity that I valued, perhaps because it only lightly colored my life.

The timing was impeccable. True to our relationship thus far: the worst time possible, yet we were both committed. We had just made the decision to live with each other, and had to live with what I felt like was an emotionally awkward and exhausting existence of residing in our home with a roommate we had asked to leave, to move out. I had taken on the burden of her inconvenience and found my spare time within the 30 days characterized as quiet tiptoes through the house. Between my two full time jobs of waitressing and teaching, I found great difficulty in setting aside time to dedicate to myself, my thoughts.

I was somewhat astounded at the steady and eloquent pace in which Rob seemed to meander through his words and mind. It seemed for each several words he proudly placed checks beside; I was barely etching visible lines. Although I was proud of him, I could not help but wonder if I would keep my end of the promise. I had committed to write regardless of what would become of us. I knew that I would finish, but I didn't know how mentally committed I could be.

The words were in the forefront of my mind, a continuous, steady and loud drumming. Every time one of our words was mentioned, I perked, I paid close attention, I listened, and I started to scribe my past. At the point that I began to write, I wrote feverishly. In a somewhat stream of consciousness manner, I let my heart pour onto the paper. In the end, the words were difficult to identify. I could not recognize myself. I suppose I had yet to take the time to truly look.

The whirlwind month was not by any means of the word "easy". I am uncertain, even at this moment, if I have ever experienced such a monumental· challenge. I have stared, dared, and taunted outsiders into the ring; but, I didn't expect this melee. I believed in my individual strength; but, I had yet to encounter this opponent. For 30 days, I dueled with myself.

In the end, Rob was right. He had foreseen the unimaginable vulnerability that we would both throw ourselves into and the possibility of irrevocable damage to our relationship.

Innumerable tears were shed, at some point we
both pushed, we both tempted to run.   Thankfully,
neither of us was willing to let go, just yet.

As I was learning the scary depths of myself, I was
meandering through his mysterious past. His stories
were insatiable to my soul. Each one of my own
painful memories was met with something spirited
from his past. Ironically, his words healed wounds
that I never knew presided within me. Both deeply
grounded and devoted to gratitude, we emerged
lightened by the weight of our past.
In 30 days: I found what I never knew was lost---
myself.

The Letters of Gratitude

The letters that follow are raw and unedited communications with self. They capture the essence of two individuals: two truths, two journeys, two unique stories of becoming. These are our words, beneath it all this is who we are, how we see, and how we came to be.

Growth

The ability to acknowledge experience, reflect and shift. It is embracing the self as a sculpture that is constantly molding and shifting into something more beautiful, more defined and more honest than the day before: utilizing our experience as a personalized teaching tool, letting go, forgiving self and being better because of it. We have all undergone moments that replay in our minds 1000 times over, reliving, scrutinizing every choice. Dabbling in the "what ifs" knowing that it was, and it was for a reason. I know that I have played with my past, rewinding, pausing, fast forwarding, re-recording. For me, it is important at some point to put the shards of my past to rest. I have learned and I have changed. I have been challenged and I have triumphed. Growth for me is the ability to truly let go. Let the past empower you to a place where it does not guide your choices, but rather informs and educates you. Growth is a place where you can look back, at where you once were and realize you couldn't flourish without it. Sow the seeds of the past, and fertilize the future. You wouldn't have grown without it, but it doesn't always need to trickle into the future. I am a fortunate to be a resemblance, rather than a replication of who I was yesterday.

Growth

We start this adventure in life as a baby: awake, alert, pure: eager to learn and explore; open and receptive to all of life's opportunities. Experiences occur, mindsets form, changes take place. Everything that happens becomes a part of us: good, bad, happy, sad. These experiences shape us; they are embedded in our hearts, minds and soul. At some point we all crave life to be what it once was, easier, more fun, to do what we want, to love unconditionally, to be accepted fully. In order to grow, we must look at where we started. Our journey of growth and search for the secret has always been with us, the simpler we make life, the better it gets. We grow up in the country and move to the city, to make a better life; only to dream of retiring in the country. We seek to be awake in this world, alert, pure, balanced and open to all great things just like when we were born. Growth represents to me a true circle of life and the choice to simplify existence by appreciating this gift.

A new baby is like the beginning of all things-wonder, hope, a dream of possibilities. Eda J Le Shan

Expectation

Predestined for disappointment; preliminary test-run of life in the mind. Calculating what should be and who should do what, often at the root of failure. Planned in a way that doesn't allow the true colors pervade expectation. Can often have a detrimental effect on the way people gauge where they position themselves in life. Alter the way they view their partners. Challenge their definitions of friendships. Calculations of whether life has been a success or not, drawing conclusions. Rating self and others on an under-examined ideal; conversely, driving people to push personal paradigms. Not allowing satisfaction to appease the being and driving self to a place beyond the recognizable scope, attempting to be better. Expectation is twofold---for me it has often been something that I hold up as an imaginary measure of success. Ideal vs. Reality. Although in the past I have had numerous occasions where I have been swallowed by the pity of my own self despair---I try to keep an open mind when it comes to others, when it comes to my life. I am at an age of uncertainty where many people are certain of what I should have, what my life should look like. For myself, I expect honesty. For others, I expect them to be honest with themselves.

Expectation

The attitude that someone should achieve, or belief that something will happen in the future. This pressure has been the downfall of many great people, and the killer of many relationships. Whether you have been on either side, chances are there has been disappointment. If someone doesn't hit the mark, both parties lose. Life is about creating win-win scenarios. I have found that the most successful and happy times have been when I have been present, where there is no pressure. I excel in these periods. Personally, when something has been expected of me and I do it, than heavier demands get thrown on me. It is important to determine what it is you want, and go for it. Be driven by desire and want. People want to succeed, be happy and enjoy life. There is no need to expect!

Support people to be the best they can be and you might be surprised at the results!

I am not in this world to live up to other people's expectations, nor do I feel the world should live up to mine.

Fritz Perls.

Trust

Belief that the intention of others is untainted by the unsavory emotions that sadly seems to drive so many people in the world. The feeling that changes as life transpires, as experiences teach, as hindsight boldly burrows itself in the mind. It is the universal challenge to believe in good, in spite of the reality that connotes the exact opposite. A choice to not allow the past to dictate the future. A choice to look at people as individuals, at people who deserve the benefit of a blank slate. Having the courage to acknowledge that we are all uniquely flawed, but deserve to be looked at as the epitome of perfection. Undoubtedly, mistakes manifest, but perhaps the only mistake is defining it as such. Opting to see it as an upward stumble, rather than a downward fall. Trust. A place I stray from constantly, but I a place

I always return to. This has been equally the root of many discouraging as encouraging events and relationships in my life. It has been and continues to be a topic that pervades every waking moment of my life. Just yesterday, I was cautioned by my father about love and in the same breath he advised me to jump in and just believe. I like to think I have faith in humanity, the intentions of myself and others. I can only control myself and any attempt at anything beyond that would result in mental devastation. I am so excited to meet my next moment, my next experience, my next embrace. Arms open---I welcome whatever wanders my way. Believe.

Trust

Truth, belief, integrity, character, respect: the tricky one in my life. Trust represents a huge range of emotions for me. I deem it very important. A cornerstone for relationships. I used to trust everyone, as the years progressed and cuts got deeper. Walls were formed. Trust had to be earned, deserved, worked for, people had to gain it. We base a lot of our life on our experiences, life was actually a lot easier and definitely a lot more fun without these barriers of protection. When it hurt, time healed it as it always does. Interestingly enough, I feel I have come full circle. Surrounding myself with good people allows me to trust, I want to trust freely again. The freshest relationship I have formed has shown me to live life to the fullest. To play, love and live. I feel my wall crumbling as my heart opens fully to walk a new journey. A risk?

Not for me. Wherever this takes me, I welcome as I

am coming to the reality that trust comes from

within and while we normally talk of trust with

others, I now acknowledge that trust starts with me.

I trust myself 100 percent

Follow your heart, but be quiet for a while first.

Ask questions, than feel the answer. Learn to trust

your heart.

Unknown.

Fear

Unknown places, emotions--- a creation of the mind driving the individual to avoid---run---disengage. A challenge, dual between the negative imagined and the calming realism of rationalism. Places unseen, experiences unlived, love un-nurtured, friendships un-flourished---steps stopped. Footsteps in the mind never having the opportunity to imprint, impress. Fear---for some people this equates to a loss, yet it seems to you first must have had it in your grasp in order to let go. Oddly, this has had so much impact on my life, my experiences, that I find it difficult to capture the collection of its effect, the way I see it in this space. Perhaps, the very resistance to the definitive in itself is explanatory. It has pushed me into the arms of people I should have ran from, into the backseat of strangers cars, into being the spectator of intravenous drug use,

into the sexual exploitation of myself, into running

and slamming the door on love. It has challenged

me to jump into freezing lakes in the heart of

winter, to dedicate my life to the education of others

and self, to drive fast, to love, to live. Fear equals a

cornucopia of experiences that I would not wish to

live without. In the face of it I am reminded I am

alive, I am awake and ready to leap.

Fear

A treacherous emotion that blinds us all at

sometime: scared, threatened, afraid, petrified. The

mind soars, the heart races. What can take us to this

place? Why did we go there? How did we get here?

The interesting thing about fear is that it is just an

emotion. One that makes us cringe but still just an

emotion. I was taught that fear is a worthless

emotion.

False

Experiences

Appearing

Real

Think that through for a moment. Fear is normally

a result of our mind running ramped. Everything

happens for a reason. It is how we choose to deal

with it. Some situations are worse than others, but

we still control how we choose to deal with and view it. The mind is a powerful tool and by knowing that you control your destiny allows you to push fear right outside the door you came from. Fear is a bully, it really is. It pushes us around if you let it and knocks us down. Look it in the eye and remember. False, Experiences, Appearing, Real. How about working on life and live in freedom every day.

Nothing in life is to be feared, it is only to be understood.

Marie Curie.

Hope

Belief in possibility. The absence of doubt. Being at peace with the unknown. Faith in oneself. Taking ownership in the things in which we do control. Giving into the beauty that lies ahead. Knowledge that there are hurdles yet to be jumped, but knowing that you will get over them. I have never been much of a person who has dedication time to faith that has which to unfold. We are the creators of our own existence---we live in a place that has been sculpted by our inner artist. If this crumbles, I do believe I have a new vision and am ready to recreate, re-sculpt out of the crumbles. When I try to think about the hand I will hold in 10 years, 5 years or tomorrow, I have no idea what that will look like. I cannot predict, nor would I want to attempt to know what actions I may take, or they emotions that may enthrall my essence, I do hope I will be honest to myself---be a wiser, prouder, bolder, stronger, more integral and beautiful person than I am today. I do have genuine hope for that which I do not control. I hope what I am, my genuine intentions shine through myself. I hope the lives that I encounter, the people I meet, love, walk by are better for that momentary glimpse, embrace. I hope I impart only a small positive impact on people. I hope to leave an imprint not easily washed away.

Hope

A new day, a new life. A bridge that carries us
from darkness to light. Some people just need to
see a glimmer in order to move forward, step by
step. My youth was very much in conflict over this.
My mother lived for hope, while it was nonexistent
in my father's vocabulary. The truth for me is that I
understand both. Emotions of pain and hurt
definitely require us hope to pull us through.
Business states that we do it or we don't, hope is for
the frail. I think that anything that provides
inspiration to people is positive. However you see
it, whatever you call it. If it works for you then run
with it. Use the bridge to get over that river and
into the light. Sometimes the warmth of the sun, is
enough to ignite your day. Even if it is just for a

brief second. Do whatever it takes. Only you know what it is.

Learn from yesterday, live for today, hope for tomorrow.

Albert Einstein.

Pain/Scar

Mend to, tend to, and ease the pain. A physical manifestation of something that has long ago supposedly healed and etched its memory on my skin. I have hid them, embraced them and created them. Tattoos mark a moment that beckoned me to feel and give me an excuse, a focus beyond my mind and my heart. Perhaps, I have always longed for and ensured a shift in power. Strike me, and beat me down. I will tattoo myself. I have always found a way to mark myself---remind myself of the road that I continually tell myself I will never again travel. Navigation has never been one of my strong attributes---they symbolize where I have been, but the places---landscapes and inhabitants I will never again encounter. I have successfully mapped my journey. The scars that splatter my body scream strength every time I gain the courage to look at the being that so clumsily dances through life. My

unexpected destinations have colored in the stencil

of my being. I know where I am going---my path is

paved.

Pain/Scar

Personal memories haunt my soul, recollection of events, defining moments. The feelings overwhelm logic at times. We've all felt it at some point in our lives, the loss of a loved one, the blow of a heavy hand, the rejection of someone we care for, an act unforgivable, another slash to the heart that cuts deep. The beauty of wounds is that they always heal. We run our fingers over the bumps, indentations of our skin. Some have the physical reminders, others … internally. I believe that pain builds character; it shows us that we can get up after we have been knocked down. We will recover… at some point. The scars of my past have brought me to where I am today. Don't be afraid of pain. Pain is nourishment. It is nothing more than a reminder of who stands before us today looking us back in the mirror. Its not the pain that we have felt, or the scars that are apart of us that determine who we are, it is how we decide to use that pain to enhance our life today. I wouldn't change a thing because pain has taught me many valuable lessons.

Pain is weakness leaving the body. Tom Sobal.

Passion

Pollute and infuse the world with unbound energy.

Letting the contagious free, unbridled by the

outcome, it satisfies the soul, it quenches the thirst,

it fills the void. Passion. For me this is such a

centrifugal force in my life, it caffeinates me in

ways that it is incomparable to anything else. I look

at my dad who explained that this is one thing that

is lacking in his life---and than he explained the

way that he sees it in everyone else. I thought to

my self, but never expressed---I see passion in his

eyes every time he makes my mom smile, every

time he makes one of his children laugh. It's in

everybody's life. It drives us forward---it ignites

the world, it creates beauty, it stirs smiles. I am

fortunate to have this for so many things: teaching,

writing, cooking, literature, conversation, hugs,

shoes, love, photos, music, and spontaneity. It is

something that I continually seek; I see so much of

it in others which inspires me to continue my quest.

To the possibilities that await me.

Passion

I remember having the opportunity to go to a seminar as a young boy of 11 with maybe a hundred people. It was training on creating wealth and the man who delivered the presentation was very passionate. Tall, lean and had strong presence. I remember distinctly 2 things: 1) he was a yo-yo champ back in the day and he demonstrated with such passion and excitement in his three piece suit his skills with two yo-yos flying around. Incredible. Secondly, was his saying "do you want to win, or do you want to be happy". I remember leaving with an uplifting feeling. The energy in the room was fantastic, I love that feeling. 25 years later, I was revisited by this great man but in a totally different arena. It was a computer download video that was recommended to me by my brother. It became a world wide phenomenon and I can't help but admire the dedication of this man. He had a message and followed his dreams all those years. From a small gathering of 100 people to being a part of a movement, really made me realize that in order to achieve greatness, you must have passion. The movie: "The Secret" the man, Bob Proctor.

Gratitude is an attitude that hooks us up to our source of supply. The more grateful you are, the closer you become to your maker, the architect of the universe, to the spiritual core of your being. It's a phenomenal lesson.

Bob Proctor

Failure

False cognitive discourse that the intended target has the optimal recourse. Consequence of solidifying the psyche in a particular outcome. When I look at the people who find themselves in disparity, people who are unnerved by the fruition of their lives---when I think about the times I have been in a place of disappointment---it has only been because the picture envisioned, doesn't fit the timeline, the precision, the lines are defined differently---perhaps blurred. This is not to say that the outcome is not right. In fact, in may be the closest moment to perfection, yet disappointment ensues, sadness evoked, tears shed. Who's to say that failure isn't the exact place you're meant to be. Kicked out of school, tests failed, jobs obtained, fired from friends---rejected. Who's to say this isn't right. A new life, a new world. I think of the women in my life, I think of the long conversations

we have had about men, about the frustrations they

have because they don't fit into the mold created in

their mind. Some gauging their success on an

imaginary timeline. I know I have set myself up to

fall because when I really stop to think about my

frustrations, times of anger, disappointment, I

realize it is because it counters my mindful creation-

--my plan. I am fortunate to have failed enough in

my life, to catch disappointment before it becomes a

reality. No plan, no place to be, no idea what lies

ahead--- I will embrace whatever lies ahead,

whatever I become.

Failure

For much of my life I have felt very close to this, the heavy lump of expectation that in my mind was heaped on me at a young age. The peacekeeper unifying a family that wasn't bondable. The promise of always keeping my mother safe, only to lose her at nineteen. To be a successful business man like my father…for many years, the many attempts of chasing what others deemed as important was high on my priority list. Realization. Non-performance of what is expected means that I am not living my life for me. The outcomes can be different….even better that what you wanted. Simpler than originally intended is where I choose to go. Being grateful for what I have, and being excited by the new day. The disappointment of others which consumed me for years, is irrelevant

now. Expectations of others lead people to believe
that we are failure, but reality shows us that if we
live each day fully, that failure is not an option and
doesn't even exist.

There are not failures- just experiences and your
reactions to them.

Tom Krause

Peace

Balanced. Teetering along the mental tightrope of life. Playing in this unscripted sanctuary. Finding calmness in the chaos. The microcosmic world in the center of the hurricane, where everything whirls around you, fast furious, on the brink of destruction; but you have your haven . Stillness, resilient to the wind. Embracing your "so called" flaws, alongside your gifts as intricately important to the masterpiece of you. Accepting the challenges as well as the triumphs. To me it is everything: it is the cornucopia of the world in its entirety. It is acceptance, welcoming the spectrum. There is always a choice---accept the reality that surrounds you, evoke change or choose a new lens to gaze through. For me its simple, I have always though of myself as a sympathetic and empathetic individual. Perhaps the biggest pain that brews in my being is for people who cannot or do not know how to find a place of peace in their life. I am constantly and consciously this place of emotional sublime. I am thankful that I have been there and know how to get back. I am forever slipping off the narrow rope, but thankfully the net beneath gently nudges me back in the right direction.

Peace

Freedom from disturbance, quiet and tranquil,
contentment and harmony. The feeling of stillness
within your mind, the calmness in your heart and
the fullness of your soul. The glimpses that have
touched me throughout the years remind me of what
we all are seeking. Unconditional love: a spirit so
free that we radiate non judgment and zero
expectations, a life of peace and filled with love,
un-boundless life and excitement. To look into the
eyes of a woman and just know. To hold my
children and just know. To live life and just know.
Freeing ourselves allows us to move into the luxury
of peace. From this day forward, I commit my life
to the simplicity of this amazing gift, I deserve it.

When you find peace within yourself, you become

the kind of person who can live at peace with

others.

Peace Pilgrim

Resentment

A word that existed on the outskirts of my discourse and something that I have grappled with throughout my entire life that I have refused to acknowledge. A negative emotion so strong that it taints the way that you view the individual, so blinded by the acts that you are able to see the person for anything other than that moment, that action, that choice. I honestly thought that I couldn't relate to this word until it was poignantly shown---I revel in resentment---I have been the cause of it, I have felt it for others, I feel it for myself. I left my partner of 10 years because of violence---I resented myself. I was harassed by an ex so often that he became known as a "lawn ornament", I resented myself. Truthfully, I do not hold any ill-conceived emotion towards anyone at this moment---I cannot, nor will I ever have the ability to control anyone other than myself. There actions towards me I cannot alter, I can however cling to the teachings of them. Don't be afraid to run, to hide, to feel, to be alone---just be and have pride in where you are and the choices made, they have contributed to you, let go of the emotion, cling to the essence.

Resentment

Anger, bitterness, ill-will, the harsh tongue, the vivid act. We have all experienced this at some point. Probably from both giving and receiving. The emotion, borderline hatred at that moment, that flings us into rage. Normally followed by justification of the severe injustice committed against us. Inexcusable, never again. Flip it. Defense to the attack. The feeling of shame for hurting someone you loved, the impulsive act that at the time felt right. The adrenalin pumping through your veins. Again...inexcusable. Never again. No matter what side of resentment you sit on, it conjures the sharp taste of pain. Short lived, or sentenced for an eternity, be still, have the ability to shift, change, adjust, realign and refocus. The biggest trick of all is clearing resentment in ourselves, our biggest critic and fan. I solute this gift for allowing me the ability to transfer energy to

a better place.

Guilt is anger directed at ourselves- at what we did

or did not do. Resentment is anger directed at

others- at what they did or did not do.

Peter McWilliams

Lust

Desire. Yearning, craving. I want, I need. It is that guttural feeling within you that motivates every action, every step. Mental obsession---physical incompletion, haunting rhythm pushing, breathing and pulsating in your being. Attainment satisfies your soul. Some people say the pursuit is always better than the achievement. I can honestly say for me this is not a truth. Although much of what I want has yet to find its way into my world, I only truly lust for what I have had. For years I kept one of the things I lust for under careful guard. Late at night in dark rooms, early in the morning, one spring birds bore witness to my well kept indulgence. Recently---busted. Out in the open, a moment of weakness, no longer privatized. I crave, I indulge. I black out. Consumed by the dark, warm, rich, sweetness. Admitingly, common but perhaps I see our relationship as somewhat different, unique, special. It is difficult to share, to throw away, to see, and smell in its unconsumed position in a nearby cupboard or drawer. I know its location at all times. My partner has tapped into this knowing the way that I see it, feel it, crave in it, indulge in it. Sometimes placed carefully in his warm palm, I have to resist grabbing it, pushing him over, and swallowing it so that I don't have to share. But I love him and I am thankful to share a taste with a man I crave nearly as much.

Lust

Overwhelming desires, extreme cravings, intense
eagerness. Hearts thumping, perspiration drips.
What takes you there? Sex, chocolate, money,
power, evolution of our planet allows the driving
desires of our heart, wallet, mind or physical being
to be there for the taking. Some like the adrenalin
rush, lots are afraid of it, or won't allow that much
energy to be expended. It's healthy to have a
desire. A passion intense that it consumes you for
long periods, on the hand it can turn to obsession.
For me, lust is a very powerful emotion, its exciting,
a huge transferral of energy, very powerful and
enticing. Intimately, it allows you to go places you
want to go. It gives you courage. It's a super
charged form of intimacy. The aphrodisiac,
chocolates or oysters. Enjoy all that it has to offer.

In our minds love and lust are really separated. It's hard to find someone that can be kind and you can trust enough to leave your kids with and isn't afraid to throw a man up against the wall and lick him from head to toe.

Tory Amos.

Shadows

Wandering in the wake of where you walked before. Your light casts a darkness clouding the vision of my steps. Blinded by the darkness of your ever persistent presence. I have little hope of ever evading the reality that I will always exist in the impressions that you have carved for me. Ignorance of your existence have left me undeniably defeated. Over the years I have struggled with the reality that I only exist because of you---in truth darkness only exists as a result of light. Biology. I am the child of someone whom I could walk past on a crowded street and not recognize. I am a child of someone I could converse with in a grocery store line up over the minuta of life and the rising costs of the staples of survival. I have no idea who you are, but I certainly know who I am. I appear to be someone who has wandered a distance to find my place here in the presence. Conflicted fruit, I am not what I

appear. Nurture, profound admirable love by a

stranger. The epitome of selflessness. Proudly I

will walk in the wake of your movements---light.

Shadows

Lurking deeply within the soul. What is there?

Hidden from light. The unknown place between

light and dark. An emotion stirring. A person

hiding. A creature ready to pounce forward. The

shadows of my past, have always been eerie. The

weak copycat of the man, that always gave me that

feeling of gloom. The dark reflection from within.

Out of darkness always comes light. Stop hiding in

your shadows, and step into the brightness of today.

Don't allow darkness to lead the way. Our shadows

are always with us. Appreciate the beauty of them.

Look for them as opportunities. Take that step

forward. Accept that darkness, respect it, and

acknowledge it. It is a part of you. Your past

present and future. Connected forever. Don't stand

there lurking in the depths of your past, or current

fears. Release them to the light and live for the

now. Be present in sunshine.

Beware that you do not lose the substance by

grasping at the shadow.

Unknown

Solitude

Strength in individuality. Unaltered by the winds that thrash against your core. Fulfillment in self, gratitude in being able to stand alone, encircled by love. Acting in accord to individual will. Taking into account the emotions of others, but being who you truly want, doing what you would do, regardless of what eyes gaze on and judge your movement or pace. Being able to see the conventions of the world for what they are--- collective ideas, consumed by individuals. Solitude--- something we are taught. I am so fortunate, so thankful to have parents that have raised me with the discourse that defiance of norms is often at the defiance of self. Alternative embraced. This is not to say that rules didn't apply, or odd choices were not scorned. But at the end of the day, they would say, "Well that's Jacq." I am confident in who I am, but I am also keenly aware that my choices are often seen as odd. To me this is indicative that I am doing something right. For along time, my life was implicitly shaped. Altered by a partner who waltzed in another world---we meandered in the liminal space between. When that finally ended, I had myself---who I had become as an individual was very different than the girl that walked in. Slowing I have been stripping away the "shoulds" of my world and getting back to the person I was. Sleeping in the grass, roaming publicly in PJs, going to bed at 5 am, eating ice cram for breakfast---Whatever I feel. Grateful, to have somewhere who loves me for that. Who embraces my idiosyncrasies, I am out of the box and I am not going back.

Solitude

The art of being with oneself has very drastically

been for me over the years. When life is moving

positively, I have found time with myself to be very

empowering. It is time to enjoy myself, my feelings

of greatness and gratitude, the flowing of

confidence running through my veins. The time to

focus on me. Almost necessary as I raise the bar to

the next level, in creating balance, in an unbalanced

world. In darker times, loneliness has dragged my

spirit and soul to places unimaginable. Creating

fear within, the aloneness, sadness and turmoil.

Delivering stories of failure and disappointment.

The contrast between light and dark becomes so

relevant in moments of being with oneself. The gift

of solitude allows emotions to flow to realms of

realism and make believe. The serenity of knowing

that we continue to grow daily and that such gifts surround us.

Language has created the word "loneliness" to express the pain of being alone. It has created the word solitude to express the glory of being alone.
Paul Tillich

Secrets

Kept locked deep within the crevices of my soul.
Shut into an intentional darkness, they seek light-
seek acknowledgement, crave existence. The
longer they are ignored, the tighter the lock, the
difficult to unleash.   The un-relentless beast refuses
to be kept in the captivity you have created. The
caged creature was never intended to be caught.
Freedom selfishness stolen by your fear. In my life
I have kept many and been fortunate enough to have
freed almost as many. Most recently, while sitting
in a dark, desolate staffroom at work, I
mechanically chipped away at the stacks of
assignments that I often begrudge as a part of my
day to day life. As my mind wandered in and out of
the depth of assessment, I entertained a
conversation with a colleague. Literature. What
words do you present to adolescents today? How

do you attempt to find words that have already been written with lives that have already lived? Have you read speak? No, what's it about? A girl who has been date raped. That happened to me --- I was drugged. The caged beast broke through the dark place it had been held captive for so long. Unlocked by a mind that forgot. Keep guard of the key that so carelessly dangled within reach. There it was, a secret transformed into a truth. In that moment I changed. After entertaining the creature in my mind for a month, after carefully presenting him to a room full of strangers. I am now grateful to see it free. I am fortunate it crept out of hiding.

Secrets

Hidden away in deep dark closets, harboring feeling of guilt, lies and pain. Holding on to them, fearing them from a loved one. For me, these always came from a negative place, it meant something was hidden. It allowed the chatter of the mind to create a monster in situations that were so untrue. It wasn't until I embraced them and acknowledged that they weren't ready to share that I felt comfort. Humans are creatures of habit. If you do what you've always done, you'll get what you've always got. Sharing and processing is a gift. By allowing people the right to take their time, to be who they are, and to hold onto whatever they want, turns your fear into tranquility. I am grateful for this lesson, as so much energy was wasted on the past. I welcome secrets and all they have to offer. Opportunity,

excitement and most importantly the ability to learn.

If you reveal your secrets to the wind, you should

not blame wind for revealing them to the trees.

Kahlil Gilbran

Rainbows

Hope. Translucent color pervades the sky and stains my mind. What if. I remember as a child looking to the sky and pleaing with the universe for something magnificent. I remember wishing for some physical manifestation to show itself and than suddenly there it was. The streaks of iridescence spoke to me---in a moment my mind shifted. I had been in a place of pain and in my mind the world shifted to show me that everything would be ok. Transition. Magic became a reality. It gave me a sense of hope and taught me that if you want something, all you have to do is ask, wish, want, and there it will be. Magic. When I see them now, I think about my experience as a child and remember how extraordinarily fortunate I am to have witnessed magic in my life. I think about the challenges I have been through, I think about those moments where your mind journeys to somewhere dark or painful, than I think of rainbows…this thought takes me to a place of happiness and hope. They tell me to change, to undergo a transition, to see all of the beautiful color in my world, to look beyond the darkness---to choose to see the light.

Rainbows

Without a doubt one of nature's true gifts to us, they bring us excitement every time. We appreciate their beauty, we look for the end seeking the pot of gold. For many years, I didn't see any, I wasn't awake, I wasn't looking. And than it happened, in a moment of reflection out she came. Vibrant colors, in all her glory. I remember that feeling and will cherish it forever. The warmth, color and excitement. At that moment I declared, I want more of this in my life. A shift came from within, it was so freeing. I see them all the time now. I create them and those feelings everyday now. I celebrate it all. Whether it is a single coin, or a pot of gold I share it with everyone in my world. Look for your rainbow, you will find it. Now the big question is, what is your pot of gold and what is it worth to you?

And when it rains on your parade, look up rather than down. Without the rain, there would be no rainbow.

Gilbert K. Chesterton

Doubt

A prediction rooted deep beneath where darkness

persists and prevents the growth. Skepticism

stealing and pilfering light---Negativity creeping

into spaces where it doesn't belong. An

unwelcomed guest that rushes in and doesn't brush

his feet. Contagious, ramifications seeded. Future

challenged. Bet---All in. Conversely, motivation.

Dabble with days----something different than

imagined. Doubt. The lack of faith in self or

others, presenting negativity and offering of

pessimism. This ever present pretence repeatedly

manifests itself in my life by both my own mind and

those that surround me. For me, this is a

motivation, pushing me to prove otherwise.

Whether the outcome is detrimental or not, I seem

to find difficulty in letting the cards lay. I think in

many regards, some of the major players in my life have caught on to this and utilized it as a tool to encourage me to walk the line. Ever since I was a little girl the word "Cant" always equated with the word "Would". I am so grateful for the positive impact that this has had on my life. I know that for many people this is not the case. I am fortunate to have been driven to a place where ultimately I am happy. Without it, I would not have a place to go everyday, where inspiration is so grand and energizing. I would do it if I wasn't paid. I know many people who wake up and go through the motions, who walk in a state of sleep. I walk very awake---proud that skepticism was thrown my way---proud to throw back proof. Proof that you hold the paintbrush that creates your own masterpiece.

Doubt

Suspended between belief and disbelief. Dubious conclusions that create fear. What role does this play in your life? We can create whatever we choose, now and forever. It has always been that way, so why does human nature query reality? Traditionally, the split has been devastating. It has allowed me to come up with nightmare stories, way worse than reality. Why? There is no explanation other than not being true to yourself. Belief is power. Doubt creates phobias and skepticism. I honor this discovery. Eliminating this is a trying exercise but the rewards are great. Raise your conscious awareness to catch doubt daily and release it immediately. Feel proud you have done it.

There is nothing more dreadful than the habit of doubt. Doubt separates people. It is a poison that disintegrates friendships and breaks up pleasant relations. It is a thorn that irritates and hurts; it is a sword that kills.

Buddha

Anger

Vibrating, consumption of darkness, a vile fluid that solidify a day, a relationship, a life. Powerful---a guise of pain. An easy alternative to the truth. A barrier to a reality that can buckle you and bend your soul. An emotion that spits fire and breathes scarring burns. It drives people to utter a discourse only reserved for enemies. Anger. Fiercely pushing people into places where you are not. Evoking dangerous adrenalin that un-relentlessly unleashes. Thankfully, it is an emotion that doesn't often enter into my life. Recently, I had a conversation with a friend about a friendship loss. In anger, both of us hid from what was too painful to experience----pain. We uttered bile, burning hurts, tearing our future. We both came to the realization that at the time it was what was needed.

Friendship severed by anger beginning to be re-sewn by honest communication and love. Oddly, as challenging as it was, it was something we both needed so we knew just as much, just how powerful friendship is. I am thankful for those moments of anger because they taught me fury rises from within---pause and question why you are hiding the pain. Anger has taught me a new level of honesty. To be proud to wear pain. To present it because the alternative is causing it on another. Being honest to your emotional states saves the severance of relationships.

Anger

The raging storm that ignites rage and fury. So passionate when raw emotion is present. I spent a long period in this state, defending, pretending, justifying my back up against the wall. Discovery for me is that anger is just a guise for fear. Combine anger and fear and you slump into the perils of denial, shame and self doubt. For me this shift came when I realized an old teaching to be true "do you want to win, or do you want to be happy". I realized that I can shift how I am feeling by going to a place of happiness. So have I mastered control of anger? Absolutely not! Anger is a habit in many regards and like any habit it must be broken. I am acknowledging anger as my reminder of where I don't want to be and I know that "it" like anything is nothing more than a choice. Why would you choose this? For you, or to place on anyone? Do you feel better being angry? Maybe it allows you to justify being right? Again I ask, do you want to win or do you want to be happy?

No man can think clearly when his fists are clenched.

George Jean Nathan

Judgment

Critical eyes burn with distain for something that does not require the callousness imparted. Conclusions reached as though the predictions are so powerful they are able to dictate the course of the world. I have judged and been judged many times throughout my life. Many of which I likely do not know, or choose to acknowledge. Although both positions are at polar ends of the spectrum, one constant chimes as truth. Both push me to be a better person, motivate me to see the world, humanity for what it is, respectful of the choices made. Move me to try and be the person beyond the scope of the illicit outlook. I choose to live in the fruition of my own choices, sparked by cynicism. Once instance had a profound impact on my life, and ultimately altered the course of who I would become--- who I am today. At a point in my life where I was spiraling out of control, playing Russian roulette with my life in the best way that I could, my aunt stared me in the eyes and said "by the time you are 18, you are going to be a single mother on social assistance". She was wrong. She was wrong likely because she said it. Her judgments became the mantra of who I would not become.

Judgment

Judgment day. So precise and final, the day of reckoning. Its now or never. Decisions waver, accusations made. So who makes the call on what is right or wrong? What is right or wrong for us? There is only one person and that is you. Judgment is nothing more than an opinion, one that may feel so righteous about. Have you ever been judged? How did that feel to you? Have you done it to others? Why? Personally, the feeling of being judged in the past has brought on a lot of self reflection and questioning of myself who I really am. While that journey is somewhat self destructive, it has allowed me later on in life to appreciate the obstacles that I have overcome and leaves a smile on my face. I look at those that did judge me, never knowing what really happened and it intrigues me. It also allows me to appreciate the fact; my life is interesting enough for people to spend so much time thinking about it. It doesn't matter what other people think at the end of the day, what is important is what you think!

Judgments prevent us from seeing the good that lies behind appearances.

Wayne Dyer.

Magnetism

Push, pull. Draw in, draw out. Extraordinary

power to have the world conspire and create your

vision. The fruition of what you will---the

manifestation of the mind into the tangibility of life.

Indulging in a place where you are able to compose

the script. Create the genre of the theatrics. Choose

the stagehands and the actors---write the story in

whatever way you want. Relinquishing and

receiving. When I think about these moments when

something challenges you in the morning and it

defines your day, or when a stranger's smile alters

your mood. I think about the power of suggestion

and all that it entails. Good or bad---our life and

our relationships are guided by our thinking. As

challenging as it may be as I navigate my way along

this unmapped course, I try to peer through a filter

of optimism, of happiness---believing in having

faith that I hit the jackpot in life because I run my

own lottery knowing everything ahead of me is

going to be beautiful, enriching and right. I too

know "the best is yet to come".

Magnetism

Drawn together, a universal force, energy. The moment when there is an attraction, worlds collide. You meet someone and just know they have it going on. Some people are very magnetic, some call it charismatic. They possess an energy that everyone wants to be around; you want to be a part of it. For every ying, there is a yang. I believe we attract people into our lives. Look around you. Is your life satisfying right now, or are you in a darker place? Look at the people in your world, like attracts like. When we address our outside influences our life changes. I have cleared my closet many times, releasing good friends, bad associates and even family from my existence. It's a tough process but very rewarding. Use your magnetism to enhance and attract people who add value to your life. Change your circles if you need to. I cherish magnetism as it opens up so many opportunities.

Attractiveness and magnetism of a man's personality is a result of his inner radiance. Yajur Veda

Depression

Uninspired by the monotony of life. Unable to see anything other than dark. Unable to feel anything close to happiness. Fake smiles. Cordial relations with everybody other than self. Surrounded by people---comfort in not having time to sit and think. Alone the mind wanders and unleashes a brutality it could never scorn on another. Words beat. Memories burn. Tortuous---impaling pain purposefully in attempts to feel. I have experience the dark dungeon of the mind. I have scaled the walls of the pits of disparity. A place I needed to fall into, so I knew I had the strength to get out of. Thankfully I have only committed to a handful of things in my life---diving deep into the depths of disparity teaches empathy for those who are in a place saturated, dripping in unpalatable pain.

Survivors---we have all survived, triumphed our own worst critic. When I was training my dog, who was a puppy at the time, I recall a poignant moment that altered the pages that were to follow. Disobedience of others is met with swift reprimand, yet when we ourselves falter in a way we deem incorrect the recourse is everlasting. We beat our scars, lashing ourselves until the original sin is beyond recognition. I no longer choose to punish myself a thousand times for a crime. I am myself only choosing to convict, not guilty.

Depression

For many years I was on top of the world, I had a great job that I loved and was acknowledged by most as being one of the best at what I did. I made good money, had so much fun. Loved my life. That all came crashing down one night. Arrested at work due to an altercation. I quit immediately after being released from jail 4 hours later. No support from my employer and was embarrassed by how everything went down. Determined to start again. A new life. I didn't want to be around people. I just wanted to create my own world. Quiet, peace and tranquility is what I wanted. The first business venture I lost 60 k. 2nd lost 40. I started gambling through desperation. I hit a pit of despair, what was I going to do? Deeper I went. Chasing pipedreams. Every quick fix, fast cash opportunities, never following through. Always beating myself up. I was a loser. I hated myself, I hated my life. I was pathetic; I got fatter, smoked more, and didn't care about anything. How had I slipped so far? Why did they not believe me on that cold dark night that changed my world and turned out my light. The fire was gone. My heart was dead, my mind frazzled. I Give Up! Than a light. A little glimmer, a little voice "you're the best daddy." Day in and out, "daddy you're the best, daddy I love you, daddy you rock." If they could see it, so could I. I will not fail them ever. Depression took me down, love brought me back. The fight, the biggest of my life. I truly honor that time because I acknowledge it as a place I will never visit again. I give thanks for showing me no matter how long you go it's just a matter of wanting to get out.

Depression is nourished by a lifetime of ungrieved

and unforgiven hurts

Penelope Sweet

Surrender

Scars cover my body and my wounded heart has

haphazardly been put back together presents to the

world a colored vignette of realities clumsily glued

together by necessity---life. Living, gazing through

the remnants of the day before. I find great

difficulty in looking through this creation un-

dictated by fear, the fragility of myself, hides

behind a carefully constructed guise of strength. At

a pace painful to watch---more painful to move---I

give in. scared to open up to the world, to show the

wounds, the casualty of who I once was, I give in.

mistakes made. Imperfect, flawed, proud, loving,

scared. In a heartbeat ready to flee---here I stand. I

stand here because giving into the chase is the only

option I have. I give into love, trust, appreciation. I

am learning the script that up until this point I have

read doesn't have to foreshadow the theatrics of the rest of my life. Pencil in hand, I am attempting to scribe my vision of happiness and being at peace while indulging in it. I am learning to surrender to myself---to be me and be proud of who that is. Eraser on hand, I surrender to love and all that it encompasses.

Surrender

Definitely a tough challenge for a lot of people including myself. To let go, to release to give in to. This is the key to moving forward. To surrender yourself and every moment of the past. Its tough. Our ego makes this so. Wanting always to be right and strong. In truth we need to open yourself to vulnerability and be receptive to who we actually are. Have faith and trust in you as a person. Allow those around you to see who you really are. To look in the mirror and like who you see. To know that you will be fine no matter what situation is put in front of you. Trust in yourself, surrender. Let go of the past. Release it graciously knowing "the best is yet to come". Give into your heart and be grateful for all that you have. Allow you mind to rest. Surrender it all and just be. When you can do this you will be truly free.

The essential surrender happens with you, it is nothing to do with anybody outside you. Surrender simply means trust. It is an attitude rather than an act. You live through trust. Osho.

Addiction

Wanting to be lost in something other than self, pushing away from the reality, running from the mirror. Choosing to be blinded in an attempt to exist in a realm where pain momentarily doesn't exist. A place where bills don't exist, where dresses fit, where your choices a difference, where love is unconditional, where you hair is in place, where you couldn't care less what people think. A place where your power is unbound. When you get back everything is just as you left it---dirty dishes in the sink, unfolded laundry in the basket, bed unmade, the same person looking back at you in the mirror--- unchanged, unaltered by your momentary steps away. Addicted to ignorance. I have been addicted, and I have watched addictions push people apart. Personally, my addiction altered the way that I look at food. My passion for the kitchen took a backseat in my life, as I did whatever I could to avoid it. Empty cupboards and bare refrigerators calmed my mind. Grocery stores were hell, as I watched my relationship dissipate into something I despised. I refocused on myself. Took a hard look at what I was avoiding. When I looked in the mirror, my reflection sickened me. Gradually, that is changing and my job and my partner have re-sparked a passion that took a long rest. I am fortunate for this struggle, so that I can truly empathize with people who also walk this road. I listening ear, a warm hug---they are not alone.

Addiction

Terminology normally depicts negativity. We think
of such things as drugs, food and gambling. All
things that have been issues in my past. Acceptance
of these times in my life, now brings me to where I
am now in my present. I think at some level we all
have addictive personalities, but what I have learnt
is addiction is nothing more than a form of release.
Focusing addictions can actually be very positive.
Becoming passionate about what you want, what
you do and how you live. All great things. What if
you focused your energy on health, life and love?
Sometime the challenging times in our lives, remind
us of the choices we made. I believe those nights of
getting drunk and going out looking for fights got
me through the passing of my mother. The right
way to deal with it? Not socially, but for me it was

something that was right. There are consequences to every choice we make in life, some good, some bad. Always good for us at that particular time. Today, I choose to make people laugh and smile. Way more rewarding.

It's all right letting yourself go, as long as you can get yourself back.

Mick Jagger

Violence

Cold steel, warm skin. A rapid tongue with roaring words rolling off the same organ that hours prior had only utterances of praise. Hot fear, ice tear. Rugged ropes, smooth skin. Disbelief and truth tango to a tempo of an ill-conceived orchestration. Betrayal-- palimpsest pain. Erasure, raped of time, of innocence. Buried memories that were never meant to surface ironically wind and weave their way from secrecy to proud certainty. For the first time in my life I have stopped running from the shadows that have so persistently followed every movement I have made. I stop. I see them. I acknowledge the darkness that I have allowed to exist paces behind myself. Embrace. Growth. I do not fear the screams that echo through my past, they reverberate beautifully through my soul. Soft

whispers in each breathe of my song.

Violence

The Goosebumps rise as the memory goes back.

The journey of a nine year old boy forced to go to a

boarding school because his mom has leukemia.

The echo of footsteps on cold linoleum, rows of

bunk beds, my new home. Scared, the tears flow

down my mothers cheek begging her not to leave

me here. Gone. Surrounded by hundreds of kids. I

never felt more alone. 2 am. Dragged from my bed

by four kids and taken to a dark hallway. Slapped,

kicked, punched. Maybe an initiation I hoped.

Pillows used to prevent visible bruising. The days

were long, the nights longer. The routine was set. I

became quiet. I stopped screaming, I stopped

crying. It made it worse. They needed the reaction.

I gave them nothing. The bruises became visible,

the cuts deeper. Bones started breaking. I felt death

knocking on my door. My eyes opened. I spoke no

more. One by one they fell, knowing that if I

dropped to the ground I was dead. They fled. I

remember standing there broken nose, cracked ribs,

missing tooth, shattered cheekbone, blood flowing

from my ear with a smile on my face thinking it was

over. I was wrong. New challenges came nearly

daily, just like in life. Different challenges, the

physical ones started to disappear, mental ones

arose. Easier? Not always, just different.

Remember that you are in control of your emotions.

Belief in yourself allows you to transition and

change your situation.

Non violence means avoiding not only external

physical violence, but internal violence of spirit.

You not only choose to not shoot a man, but you

refuse to hate him.

Martin Luther King Jr.

Conform

Walking along a pre-paved path and finding a place

predetermined. Sheep. Monotony, trotting

gracefully. Pace and placed safely amongst others.

Easily opting for the choices that are accepted and

surrounding rather believing enough in self to act.

Individuality---action that mirrors the thought and

belief of the person. For many people, individuality

is an impossibility, not an option. Driven by fear,

the possibility of consequences. Why push the

boundaries when existence within the parameters is

so easy. Clinging to normalcy---fear of social

stigmas, doing what is right. Holding pseudo

psychology text as biblical words, googling "good

relationships", "true love" and "ideal weight" as

though someone other than themselves has more

knowledge than they. I suppose we have all been in

a place, where fitting in has meant disregarding individual thought and belief. I have been there more times than I am able to count. Truthfully, individuality is an impossibility and that frightens me. In the end I am thankful for the mirror of humanity, it is always easier to see the faults of self by gazing at another. Thankfully the world presents the truths, reflections of your being in infinite ways. See, acknowledge, awaken, than exist.

Conform

I always chuckle when I hear this word and the rebel comes out to play. The dictionary says "behave according to socially acceptable standards". This opens up to conversations of what is acceptable in today's society. Pretty much anything goes as far as I can see. I guess the question that I ask is are you comfortable in you as a person, or do you feel the need to have approval from everyone around you. There is no right or wrong. There just is. If you want to rock out tattoos, color your hair blue, work crazy hours and have fun, does that mean that you are treated differently than the suit wearing traditional 9-5er that makes 40 k a year and is miserable? Society, traditionally says yes. Is that right? It is important for you to express yourself for you and not worry about others. Life's too short, live life to the fullest, have fun, be crazy. Enjoy all of life's great opportunities, be respectful to people and that's all people. Conforming because it socially acceptable is a poor excuse for living. The laws of the land are the laws of the land, even a lot of those are questionable. I am talking about being in integrity with yourself, and doing what makes you happy.

I think a lot of people have lost respect for the individual, you don't know the individual, the person who doesn't conform.

Eryka Badu

Reflection

Honoring and respecting the gift of life and self.
Momentary homage's to the past, tributes to the
truth. Having faith in all that falters stumbles and
stances. Knowing that where we find ourselves, is
far more than just chance. Introspection of self and
surrounding to create meaning. To learn, to grow.
To walk a path you have yet to pave. For a long
time, I guided my next step, disregarding my past.
Believing that it all begins here and now, I
experienced many similar challenges, found myself
surrounded by similar people, different names, new
faces, but essentially the same. It wasn't until I
starting believing there was merit, meaning and
wisdom in the choices of my past that the world
around me started to shift. The once off kilter life,
has balanced to a place where when the waves

crash, I have a sturdy enough stance to not stumble

so hard. The past several months, I have been

swallowed into the depths of my psyche---

rediscovering wounds that I thought were washed

away. I have realized this has been all in

preparation for who I am meant to be---me.

Reflection

To look at oneself and life proves more challenging

than at first glance. Allowing oneself to explore

your life, a time or situation is vital for balance and

growth. The biggest thing presented to me over the

years is to differentiate between reflection and

judgment. Defined as "a thought or an opinion

resulting from such considerations" reflection

allows us to access what we have done, how we did

it and brings us to realizing of where we can take it.

It is a valuable tool when utilized in the right way

and one that can flip you on your head, and turn

your whole world upside down if you don't. Yours

must come from a place of calmness, as this will

lead to clarity and balance. I reflect all the time. I

have my magic spot that takes me to the place I

desire and deserve. A lot of people are scar3ed of

looking at themselves and their surroundings. Find

peace in yourself and all that flows through you. (I

am grateful for the gift of reflection, as it allows me

to be true to myself and create a better me.

A little reflection will show us that every belief, even

the simplest and fundamental, goes beyond

experience when regarded as a guide to our

actions.

William Kingdom Clifford

Liar

Denial of truth. Ignorance of reality. Push. Walk, run, hide, but persistently profoundly, painfully, the truth will stalk your every movement. Regardless of the world that you manifest in your mind, the landscape that you manufacture will only be an aesthetic guise for what lye beneath. Truth--- only a short time ago two truths that had been eroding in me scurried to the surface of my reality. Denial became an impossibility.

1) Tea reading...fear, hidden, buried, secrets resurrect. Death- I caused a death. Selfishness or selflessness. Abortion

2) Haunting flashbacks---pretend it never happened. Words leap from my mind through my mouth and the truth gallantly sprint freely.

The truth was always something that I clung to, hugged to and never wanted to let go of. Hug so hard, circulation would cause it to cease to exist. Cold. Lifeless, exhausted. Exasperated my arms weaken, I let go. The truths held within my warm safe embrace, diffuses into that which exists around me: warmth and acceptance meet the arrival. Departed from the depth of me and slowly swallowed into my surroundings. I have learned that keeping the truth clasped within the parameter of my arms robs me of a warm and honest embrace. The caged bird that once sat silently behind the bars of denial now sings a new song---freedom.

Liar

One of the hardest things for me to understand in

the past. Why would someone repeatedly make

false statements that create web of lies so thick and

complex? Taking them to a place that you have to

lie about the lie. The web gets stronger ... thicker

... The challenges that they encounter must be

a mind tripping experience. I have seen people

create webs that are so complex that they stretch

through the lives and minds of distanced people.

Like most I have been caught in that web

before. I've been guilty of protecting someone from

pain by adjusting the truth to soften the blow. This

then shifts to the discovery of interpretation. What

if you dream of a situation to be good when its not.

You want it to be great but realistically its not. So

how do we clarify in our minds as to what is true or

not. Intention plays a huge role in what defines a

person and their actions. Liar ...Always wrong? Many think so. I now challenge what if distorting the truth came from a place of good? The reality for me in my experiences is that nothing is more powerful than being honest with myself and everyone in my world. The truth may hurt but if it is honest then I believe that only good can come it. I keep looking for what lesson can I find in this experience. I now appreciate the opportunity to change my thought process from something of complete negativity and despise to knowing that we choose to be who we are and every decision has a consequence.

It's hard to believe a man is telling the truth when you know you would lie if he was in his place.
Henry Lewis Mencken

Time

The one constant that ties humanity and the natural

world, yet the most complex. As a child the space

between the ticks and the tocks stirred me as I

awaited each passing moment. I longed for the

sound that symbolized something new, something

exciting. Waiting for something inconceivable to

wash up on shore. Slowly, gently, loudly and

proudly it passes. Monumental moments of my past

have either scurried along at a momentum I could

hardly keep pace with, or defied my mind as

seconds barely pass when all you want is another---

to be somewhere else, another day, another hour.

Anything but the present. The gift of presence.

Perhaps the very first time in my life I was truly

present, that is not wandering in my mind to regrets

of the past, things to do today, or worries for my

future --- was when I was hiking the West Coast

Trail. I was 22 and was walking along a beach and

this man said this was his third time making the

trek. He explained that it was the only time he

lived in the moment, the only place that forced him

to think about the step he was taking. That

conversation was a gift. For me time continues to

seemingly shift---defy reason. A minute, an hour, a

day---In love, it passes so quickly that it escapes me

in a way that defies rationality. For once, I want my

life to slip away and enjoy every minute of it.

Time

The healer of all wounds. The duration that moves us from the past, through the present, into the future. Truly irreversible. There are many people who fear this free flowing monster. For stealing moments of life, while others embrace it and cherish its numb effects on life. For those caught in the past, the challenges of memories, force us to live in a world of once was and must face that. Before they know it their entire life has slipped away. For the others that dream of what will be, the future appears big of what they wish. The downside is many dreamers, live in what will be without any action behind what they want. BECAUSE THEY BELIEVE IT WILL JUST HAPPEN. Having been privy to both, I am now accepting that it is so important to be in the now. The only place where for a brief second you control it all. Honor it, live

it.

Respect the past, prepare for the future, with action

in the present.

Rob Martin

Inspire

Skin emblematically imposed and intoxicated with

excitement. Vibrations smolder, unable to contain.

Energy transposed, diffused, consumed, recycled.

Watching the actions, hearing the words.

Rendering audience motivated, rejuvenated--- left to

regroup, reassess and disregard any previous

refrain. Inked soul, tattooed mind---the energy

impressed visually colors the canvas of the being.

Appreciative of the wisdom, being able to see

unblended by the lenses they looked through

yesterday. Etched mind, painted soul caressed by

the presences of serendipitous surroundings.

Inspired. I am constantly moved, reenergized by

the wondrous beings that circulate in my life. Their

stories, their snapshots of self tint my voice and

help script my steps. In moments of uncertainly,

sadness, pain, I look to my mom, my dad, the

children that fill the classroom, my friends, my

brother, my love. I see and think about the winds

left in the wake of where they walk. Collectively,

the strength, purity passed and language reverberate

through me and quietly challenge me to be an

individual. A life uprooted from doubtful glances,

rejecting the unwelcomed loud voice of judgment.

Opt for self, opt an unscripted schedule and

languish the love, laughter and life that delicately

garnish.

Inspire

I love it! Everything about it! To inspire, to be inspired. A huge driving force, the urge to do something creative. This to me is the greatest gift that I can give and receive. Such emotion is felt on both levels. Feels good tapping into yourself. The realization that we live in a fantastic time and place. Energized by others, being energized. I come to this place right now though this gift, inspired by my partner to share what is real, to share my truths and beliefs, to free myself completely. There is so much good to focus on and to believe in. I don't understand how "we" and that's myself included just don't flow with life. It is a gift that we need to appreciate more, to be involved with more. To make that difference and not be afraid. To walk it, like you talk it.

Thinking too well of people, often allows them to be better than they otherwise would be. Nelson Mandela

Laughter

Lightens the seriousness, changes a day, essential to love, binding spaces that could have never collided. Swallowed in silliness, caressing and dancing with smiles, easing tensions, creating bonds, solidifying relationships, healing heart: laughter, it is a core aspect of my life. When I think back to times that I would characterize as challenging----it seems that uplifting quality of laughter was busy playing in another park. It is truly the ability to reflect on what is important. Is that bad mark really worth a whole day of frowning? Does that extra 5 pound reading on the scales really result in scowls? Was scuffing your favorite pumps really that big of a deal? Probably not! Contagious, even when something isn't really that funny. It has the overwhelming ability to change a course of a day, a relationship, a life. Therapy for the soul. If the theory hold a dogs tail up and he will be happy holds true, than why not with us. Consciously, something I testify to do even more of. Laugh, be funny, have fun. In twenty years when I look in the mirror, I want to see smile lines so deep they take me back to every day that I have lived. Not a moment, a lifetime.

Laughter

The missing link in so many lives, and definitely mine over the last few years. I look back to times when I was back at my best: strong, invincible, and full of life. Laughter was always present in abundance. This is the undoubtedly the biggest gift you can share with the world. It can pull anyone from the slumps of despair, and bring a smile to ones face that radiates from deep within. For many years it was my job to make people laugh and show them a good time. At some point I took a detour which took laughter from my existence and it definitely changed my world. Life was serious, not fun. I went from being the life of the party, to being a fly on the wall. The choice to take this road is still a mystery to me. I am very glad to have returned laughter to my universe. I surround myself with better situations, funnier and less serious people.

Changing your environment is sometimes all that it

takes. Do whatever it takes to enjoy the gift of

laughter. It is medicine for not only yourself, but

also anyone who is fortunate to be in your presence.

At the height laughter, the universe is flung into a

kaleidoscope of new possibilities.

Jean Houston

Love

Universally sought. Binding, weaving, gluing

together cultures and times. Symbols unbroken

encircles the being. A force that continually defies

what had been previously defined as truth. Pushing

the paradigms constructed, remolding the structure,

carving intricacies, creating a vision beyond the

depths, beyond the beauty created in the mind.

Undeniably present----it alters the course. It

navigates you to destinations you never intended to

go. You find yourself where you are meant to be.

Love. Felt deep within my core, and uttered

through my mouth. Ironically, something I thought

I was fighting for for years. Struggling to hold

onto, something that narrowly escaped my grasp,

something we falsely created. Hindsight is a gift. I

am fortunate for the lens through I look today---At

this moment, starkly, I realize love is not something

to fight for or with. Love is not cold steel, warm

skin. It does not scar you with shame. Gratitude.

Today, I feel it through my as it pulsates through

my ever present being. It encircles me with

intensity, with heat. It challenges me to speak a

language I didn't know could exist in the realm of

my voice. I have been awakened by someone, who

I am proud to walk with, someone I am in awe of,

someone I admire in a way I find difficult to define,

someone whose silence doesn't evoke an

unexplainable fear. When I look at Rob, I see him,

I feel him. A Rock---you vibrate through and

through me---I have been struck.

Love

Flowing like a mighty river with such strength and power. Unconditionally given by my mother and the gift forwarded to my children from my heart. When anxiety builds, the insecurities of relationships past, still running through my veins, I look at challenges faced. Two very different worlds have collided together, there is no mistake, its fresh, exciting, scary, loving, passionate. I quiver as I write, my mind finally slows. I feel warmth again and appreciate the brightness of each day. I have loved twice in my life, I am thankful for the second opportunity. It is here and it is real, I welcome the future. I adore the present, I am grateful for the past. Today my heart races daily, I see her, all of her. The excitement, when I see the loving smile, feel the squeeze of the best hug, hear those sweet words from her lips. I am blessed to embark on this journey, with a woman who supports me fully and makes me want to be a better man. She encourages and inspires me daily. Beautiful beyond words, her twinkling eyes ignite my soul, her smile brightens my life and the essence of her being for me is the kindness of her heart. I feel love, I am loved, I can love again.

You know you're in love, when you can't fall asleep because your reality is finally better than your dreams.

Dr. Seuss.

Creating Your Letters of Gratitude: An Emotional Guide to Your Written Experience

Writing the *Letters of Gratitude* will undeniably change your life and the way that you see the world around you. This is a challenging expedition of self that when explored honestly reveals the true essence of whom you are. Finding yourself is not an easy feat

It takes courage to keep moving forward. Although challenging, this is an extraordinary discovery and the excitement and adrenalin pushes to the surface as you uncover what was deep beneath the rubble of life---you. Beneath the language, life and experiences you have lived; beneath it all, the true you remain intact. Ready to breathe again, and ready to meet the world. You will find yourself staring someone that may be difficult to recognize. The *Letters of Gratitude* is tool that cleanses the soul; it washes away that which makes us difficult to discern to ourselves. It unties the emotional weights of past experiences, so that you can move freely, lightly and honestly in your new world. On your road to attaining personal, you may find yourself questioning where this is going other than ripping buried truths and reopening wounds that we had originally believed to be healed. In essence, they had just been covered by mountains of emotions that had allowed us to stagger forward to where we stand today: a battered solider of life. It is here and now that you have an opportunity to release the true spiritual warrior within.

You will feel a full array of emotions as you embark

upon this journey. You may even find your book

being flung out of a car window at some point.

Allow yourself the opportunity to gently put on the

brakes. Stop, reverse and pick up where you left off.

Your spiritual warrior will always step forward in

these moments, allow them to show themselves.

Creating Your Letters of Gratitude: A Practical Guide to Your Written Experience

Creating your individual *Letters of Gratitude* and capturing your own story of becoming is most successful with some practical guidelines. This practical guide is central to completing what will prove to be a life changing process. So let's get to it.

Before you get started you will need:

- Journal: we found that having a journal worked best for both of us. Originally, it started with notebooks, or typing on the computer. It is important that you feel your pen connecting with the paper. The pen acts as a conductor and a creator of your mind, emotions and psyche. A pen also creates a commitment between you and your words. Words that are not easily erased with the simple push of a button. It is almost like an escape in getting back to that time when writing actually meant something. When we write to the pace of our pen, it is an honest mirror or your thinking.

- Pen: do yourself a favor and get yourself a good pen. When writing with an instrument that feels good, you will find that your writing is more fluid. It is the instrument of your inner voice.

- A writing space that works for you: a key to unleashing your creativity and honesty begins by finding your own writing space. This will be a space for you to honor to your process. It will change constantly. We have written at various beaches, coffee shops, our kitchen table, in our car, on couches, beds, patios, on a log, and in the lawn. The place is really wherever you can be alone with your thoughts. Many times we have changed spots while writing on a word. Listen to yourself, and the place will find you. If you hit a block, change your space and automatically your feelings will change. Always welcome the change.

- The Words: Keep this list handy, or better yet memorize it. Essentially, they are the topics for each of your letters. For us, the words were constantly is our minds as we scribed our way through the 30 days. It is interesting when people use these words in daily conversation, your mental conception

of the meaning shifts

1) Growth	16) Doubt
2) Expectation	17) Anger
3) Trust	18) Judgment
4) Fear	19) Magnetism
5) Hope	20) Depression
6) Pain/ Scar	21) Surrender
7) Passion	22) Addictions
8) Failure	23) Violence
9) Peace	24) Conform
10) Resentment	25) Reflection
11) Lust	26) Liar
12) Shadows	27) Time
13) Solitude	28) Inspire
14) Secrets	29) Laughter
15) Rainbows	30) Love

GETTING STARTED

The Concept: 30 *Letters,* on 30 Words, in 30 Days.
Write honest letters to yourself, each entitled with
one of the selected words. Write your truthful
thoughts and experiences of this word and conclude
your *Letter* by gazing through a lens of gratitude,
learning and growth.

A Few Guidelines:

-Honesty: be brutally honest with yourself. This is
where you share what you would not normally share
with others, or perhaps even have the courage to
ponder yourself. Do not be afraid to visit places
that have been long forgotten or hidden deep within.
In fact, push yourself to enter into the arenas in
which you least want to go.

-Complete Each Word: finish the word you have
committed to before moving on to the next one.

-Order of Writing: you can choose any of the 30 words to write on. You do not need to go in any particular order. But when you do pick your word it is important to stick with it. Some words took us 30 minutes, while others took us 3 days. It does not matter the length of time, just be true to your word. Be present. If you hit a block, take time to reflect. There are many ways that you can spin a word. Do not take the easy road or detach from the word. Rather embrace it and explore it for yourself.

-300 Word Maximum: there is no luxury of dancing around a word, as we tend to do in the conversations of real life. Get to the point. If you are done in 150 words and your letter is complete, so be it. This naturally evolves the more that you write. For instance, Rob's first letter was over 500 words, but when the fluff was alleviated and he got to the point, it was only 200 words. These are your pages. This is your time to honor and celebrate your individual history and dive deep within who you are. Go for it.

-Believe in the Monument of the Moment: it does not matter if what you are writing at the time makes no sense at all. If it comes from within, it is right and as scary as this may sound it will all makes sense once you have completed your 30 words. It takes courage to be introduced to new facets of yourself that you never knew, or wanted to know existed. Embrace the stranger within, trust that this intricate part of yourself, and be grateful for this new encounter.

-Progress Forward: another point to take note of, when you have finished your letter move on to your next word. Do not revisit it, as there is time allocated for you to do that later. Instead, release it from your thoughts and move on. There are no restrictions to how many words are done in a day. You may find you are inspired to write 3 words in a day, but on the other hand, do not be surprised if you cannot look at your journal for the next 5 days as you will have so many thoughts running through your head. Remember, there is no right or wrong.

-The initial 30 days is an individual journey: refrain from sharing your *Letters* until you have completed all 30. We encourage you to discuss your emotional experience, but not the content.

-Commit to yourself: this is a commitment to rediscovering yourself through the scope of gratitude, 30 *Letters* on 30 words in 30 days. However you decide to do it is up to you. The only stipulation is that you honor your commitment to yourself. Write up a personal commitment in the front of your journal which reads:

Commitment to Self,

I_____ agree to write 30

Letters of Gratitude in 30 days. Starting

on_____ and finished on, or

before_____. By

signing this, I acknowledge that I will be personally

better for completing the process. I deserve to

honor and celebrate myself through this agreement.

Signed _____

Date_____

By signing this agreement you consciously and

subconsciously commit to yourself. For many of

you, like us, this is a big commitment.

Questions to Consider When Writing Your

Letters:

-How do you define this word? What does it mean
to you?

-What emotion do you feel when you hear the
word?

-What experiences, people, conversations, scenarios
have shaped your thinking about this word?

-How do you connect to this word personally?

-Where do you go to in your personal history when
you think of this word?

-How has this word impacted those around you?

-What is your honest belief of this word?

-How has this word shaped my thinking?

-How has this word evolved into my being?

-How do other people define this word?

-How can I be grateful for this word and all that it encapsulates to me?

-What would you like this word to look like in your world?

The most important part of your *Letters* is acknowledging the lessons that you have learned through your experiences and being able to openly express this. Write honestly and come to a place in which you are able to see the word through a lens of gratitude. Every experience is opportunity for us to grow, to share and help others, to create a new landmark in our lives. There are lessons and opportunities in every experience, no matter how fantastic or horrific we feel at that time. Do not ever be afraid of gratitude. Welcome it and welcome it into your letters. You are now invited to write your letters and embark on a journey that will change the course of your life forever.

See you in 30 Days

Listen to Your Words: After your 30 Day Writing Challenge

Congratulations for fulfilling your commitment to yourself. Now that you have written your letters, you probably have a lot of questions. Calm the voices in your head as this is completely normal. This time is very important. Acknowledge these letters where you were when you wrote in this journey. Read them free of judgment and expectation. Read them as they are and for what they are. Accept the letters in their entirety; they are an extension of you.

Listen: For those who had an Individual Journey

-You need to allocate approximate 90 minutes of quiet time and preferably you do this on a day that you can spend the remainder of the day dedicating to self.

- Although this process is an individual journey, we challenge you to share your letters with someone who you feel you are comfortable with and would benefit from a better understanding of you. Sharing is an important part of the process of releasing the past and committing to your new position of gratitude. If you do not have someone you feel comfortable sharing your letters with check our website for alternatives. It is at this time that we ask you to read your letters aloud.

-Read each letter individually and in the order provided: at the end of letter take some time to digest what is written. This is a time where you

need to take a moment to pause and reflect on what
has been written.

-We suggest using the remainder of the day
dedicating to you. What you choose to do is
entirely up to you, but it was important for us to
change our space and truly absorb what has been
written.

Listen: For those who Shared a Journey

-You need a minimum of 2 hours quiet time and
preferably you do this on a day that you can spend
the remainder to the day together free of
distractions.

-It is at this time that we ask you to read your letter
aloud to each other

-Read each letter aloud in the order provided. In
turn, alternate reading each letter. After the

reading, digest the letter for what it says. These are

your *Letters,* and this is your process. When we

read our letters we did not verbally converse at all.

Apart from the reading of the *Letters* we did not

discuss the content at that time. Rather, we

absorbed each others *Letters* for what they were and

accepted them in their entirety for a part of the

individual who sat before us. This was a time

defined by laughter, admiration, inspiration, with

tears shed, tissue boxes passed, and too many warm

embraces to count. We shared ourselves completely

and it was imperative for us, as it is for you, to

remain completely accepting of the *Letters.* Be free

of assumptions, and listen with your whole heart.

Regardless of your history with this person, to be

this vulnerable with another is a true act of courage.

-We suggest using the remainder of the day to be

with one another. What you choose to do is entirely

up to you, but it was important for us to change our
space and truly absorb what we had shared and
learned.

Once you have read your letters take the next 7 days
to digest. Acknowledge the words in your world.
Every time you use or hear the words, take a quick
look at the used word. What context is it in? What
lesson can you learn from this word at this point in
time? Look at the word through the lens of
gratitude. Listen to the people around you, watch
them, and learn from them. How does their
interpretation of the word affect you? Can you shift
it to gratitude? Do you choose to? Words that had
previously had a negative impact on you will shift.
Interpretations of what you deemed positive will
truly ring true for you. At the end of your seven
days you have writing exercise that will take

approximately 45 minutes. For us it was a lot quicker. In actual fact, the quicker the better because you are allowing your source to answer for you and there is no thinking involved. If you shared this journey with someone, do this at the same time.

Projecting Gratitude into the Future

Write all of the 30 words down on a sheet of paper and write 1-2 sentences explaining how you see this word through the lens of gratitude.

Simply ask yourself:

What does this word look like to you now?

How do you want to experience this word in the future?

Take as much time as you need within a 45 minute timeframe to complete the 30 words. Once completed, read what you have written. How do you now feel about these 30 words? Do you feel a shift from where you were? Through the course of writing, digesting, acknowledging and acceptance, you have created new landmarks for your life. A landmark is a new marker or reference point that as a result of the *Letters* has now shifted. Take a look at an experience that you encountered in your past and wrote about. Before, whenever you revisited an experience, it would bring up certain feelings and emotions pertaining to the actual event. Those feelings have probably remained the same for many years. Now that you have written about this experience or event and have shared your gratitude for the lessons learnt, you automatically shift. Every time you now revisit this event, you are now grateful. When you slip into your past, you will always come back to being thankful. This is a new landmark you have created for yourself. Creating new landmarks allow you to advance your past dramatically. When this happens you move yourself closer to the present and living in the now. Essentially, you have created a new you. It opens your awareness, and shift the way you see the world. It allows you to create new commitments with yourself and release old habits of thinking that have been self destructive in the past. Creating new landmarks is like creating new software in the brain, it allows you to smarter, to be faster, to alleviate viruses that you could not with your old software package. Simply speaking, your old landmarks were outdated. They meant you were slow and could not remain current. The more you resisted growth the deeper you would slip. You are now current! Your landmarks are fresh. This creates clarity, knowing that you are armed with simple tools to move forward. Remaining in a state of

gratitude is a continual process. Constantly

updating your landmarks, will be a ritual that you

will love, it is very satisfying. You will have a new

reference point that keeps changing as you do.

Projecting Gratitude into the Future: Page by Page We Weave Our Words

The following statements are mantras for self. They were created is a somewhat stream of consciousness manner and answer the question: how do you want to see this word in our future? Side by side, Rob and Jacq, projected their vision for the future and weaved together their thoughts. As a unified voice: these are the lenses they commit to see through.

Growth is the best part of life. Planting life seeds and making positive agreements with self allows us to blossom a little more each day. It is the belief that the individual is fluid and ever evolving; embracing self through all the changes.

Expectation of self or others is the greatest of all evils. It is the ultimate parasite of life that sets you on a road of destruction. When you lose expectation, you gain happiness. Ultimately, by embracing the entire world has to offer as an unknown, you can only be pleasantly surprised.

Trust is the complete belief in self. Ultimately, it is having faith that what is, is what is right.

Fear is an allusion that slows progress. It is a firm push in the right direction. When we look closely, reality repeatedly demonstrates that there is absolutely nothing in the world to fear, especially self. Thank you.

Hope is the ever changing gift of creating your dream life. It is the vision of what you will see tomorrow.

Pain is something we believe to be real, but it is nothing more than we create for our self. Ultimately, it can remind us of the road we have walked and serve as a proof that people continually emerge better than they were the day before.

Passion drives us to be the best we can be with whatever it is that you choose to do. Act in accordance with what sparks your soul.

Failure is the gift of learning of what does not work and shows us better ways to succeed. It is a lens which is unnecessary to see through and it provides an opportunity to reassess and choose to only see the triumphs.

Peace begins and ends with self. We must honor it, than share it. To be truly at peace, we must learn to accept and love everything that surrounds us--- including self.

Resentment is nothing more than not trusting. It is an emotional projection that unwittingly reveals what we most want to change about our self. We must believe the emotions we chose are exactly

right at that time and have the wherewith-all to see

what lies beneath.

Lust is a powerful emotion; it is the desire that

drives us so instinctually to amazing realms of our

world. Peruse what pulsates within and embrace

the moment when it is before you.

Shadows are true opportunities to find light and

love by looking away from the dark. To find this

we must live honestly and cast the all revealing

light of truth on the world; a place where shadows

cannot exist.

Solitude is the ultimate gift of love to self. Sharing

time with ourselves allows us to love, learn and

grow.

Secrets provide moments of false security. They act as a looking glass that if we have the courage to gaze into reveals what we are most ashamed of. If you had the real courage of honesty, you can share yourself entirely with the world and open the door to opportunity.

Rainbows allow light and magic into our worlds. It means opening your eyes and seeing the real magic that occurs everyday.

Doubt comes from deep within. It is self destructive and a complete waste of time. When you learn to alleviate doubt, you will be able to flourish in the beauty of "now". Life truly awards you with what you believe it will.

Anger equals confusion through assumptions. When we ask questions to clarify, anger dissipates. It is an emotional sign to look deep within self and heal what hurts.

Judgment is the biggest waste of energy on the planet. Release the judge inside of you and watch the victim walk away. It is an unnecessary projection on the world. We must learn to accept others and their choices as perfect for them.

Magnetism connects like with like, it is powerful, yet so natural. When you believe in it, you can draw your individual dream and allow the world to color in your vision.

Depression is a choice. When that is what we opt for, it shows us that life is only going to get better

than where we are. That is definitely worth
celebrating.

Surrender to all that has been, give in to the world
for the lessons it offers and release
everyone and choose a path of happiness.

Addictions are nothing more than masks of fear
which we know are not real. They are a sign from
self to look deep within and question what you are
hiding from. Nothing is better than the gift of life
seeing through a clear lens that is vibrant and true.

Violence is weakness on all levels. It can provide
an opportunity to grow where we can shed the skin
of who we were the day before. To be a spiritual
warrior we throw love on

Conform to the beliefs of a happy self and watch your world change. To be a true individual one must act according to their own truth, even if it means standing alone. Solo honestly is far more powerful than a collective lie.

Reflection allows us to see who we really are. It is a reflective and shiny key that can unlock who we are deep within and reveal the purpose of our path; cherish the mirror inside enjoy what you see.

Liar represents not being honestly present. Respect yourself and be true to your word. Proudly offer your authentic self and at the same time embrace others for who they choose to be and what they offer.

Time never stops, nor should we. How we choose to use it is perfect for us in this space. It is a valuable gift that we should share lovingly with people and experiences that reflect individual aspirations.

Inspire is to be true and acknowledge all that you are and to share all of you. It is that energy found deep within self that is constantly visible if you choose to see it.

Laughter frees your soul and brings joy to all. Choose to be lighter and give into the contagion of happiness.

Love is the true source of life where everything begins. Love yourself completely without judgment and be free. By loving ourselves in our entirety, we can embrace others for all that they are.

The Effect: An Altered Discourse

We are extremely grateful for the process of dedicating and exploring our true selves. It has enabled us to open our lines of communication fully and has enhanced not only ourselves but our relationships with each other and to the world. We are free of any inhibitions or fear. We have positioned ourselves in a place that is full of love and where we have freed ourselves from our own judgment and from the judgment for others. By offering our true self to the world, we have shed that which has traditionally hindered progression forward. Our masks are off and we are able to expose ourselves fully and express honestly what we desire for the future. *The Letters of Gratitude* have completely opened our minds to living in the

now and creating what we hope for the future today.

The following are gifts we received from going

through the process of the *Letters*.

Releasing negative people and all the unwanted emotions attached to them:

-Recreating relationships in a way that is positive for you.

-Filtering in positive language and sharing loving words, opposed to judgmental thoughts.

-Helps you understand the influence of other peoples language on your own psyche---who is good for you and who is not.

-Strength without guilt to free yourself which sometimes means letting go those who you love but acknowledge are not positive in your world.

Create Landmarks of Optimism

-freeing the negative emotions attached to situations of your past. This enables you to see these experiences as integral to your individual story of becoming you.

-allowing negative experiences of old to become important lessons that you appreciate for having informed you and providing you with an opportunity to grow.

-Recreating your past and finding an optimistic platform to stand on, as opposed to where you were and how you used to feel.

Appreciation of Self and Others as Complex Individuals

-creating feelings of self worth, rather than self destruction.

-seeing the world with less judgment because we have a better understanding of ourselves and others

-empathy of others because we can acknowledge that if we have a complex story of who we are, than we can see others as complex and have story behind who they are and how they behave.

Communication

-being more open with your personal history leads to daily truth and honesty.

-Once you have been honest with yourself, this naturally leads to being open and honest with others.

-Sharing the genuine being behind the masks: feelings and hidden truths suddenly emerge and become imminent to share with those around you.

-a strong desire to seek resolution, and learn about the individual behind the words

Lessons in times of Challenge

-when difficult scenarios or people are encountered, they are viewed as teaching tools that will lead to a better you. The question continues to arise "what will I learn from this?"

-Logical reason supersedes any natural emotional response.

-Ability to be objective with other peoples challenges, rather than jumping their "emotional bandwagon"

Use words more Carefully

-Words become more than just words. They become a powerful tool that can be either or positive or negative. The true impact of words is the change in the interior dialogue you have with yourself.

-allows us to present our thoughts with more clarity: essentially we understand the value in thinking before speaking. Think. Reflect. Speak.

-Understanding our own complex use of language, you will have the urge to seek clarity in other people's language.

Overall Sense of Optimism

-entrenched in a language of gratitude leads to a shift in thinking that allows us to create something positive in every situation.

-the belief that everything will is as it is meant to be and accepting that whatever happens is right for you at this particular time.

Listen to the Words:

Words are the gateway between safety and

vulnerability, self and others, past and future---the

space between. We wear a mask of safety when we

choose to hide from vulnerability and not offer our

authentic self to the world. Often language is mask

that we haphazardly wear over who we truly are.

Although we share a common language, a unified

mask, we all uniquely see through it; as it is shaped

by our lives lived, as experiences occur, as words

are spoken. We behave in accordance to the way

we view words. Words manifest thoughts, thoughts

stimulate action, action creates progress, and

progress is growth. Our expression and

understanding of language is constantly a

compromise between who we once thought we were

and who we have become. Yet our vocabulary and

way of expressing ourselves to the world is

constant. How is it that we are continually evolving as individuals, shifting our thinking about what words mean to us, and we continue to speak in the same way? *The Letters of Gratitude* is a necessary pause in life: an opportunity reflect and capture who you have become. This is a path that will guide celebrate and understand your unique stories as an individual. When we ourselves bring to light our own complex use of language and ways of seeing and understanding the world, we are better able to see the world around us with compassion and empathy. Developing the depth of words and understanding what these words really mean to you, will open an honest line of communication with world. Behind each conversation is an individual truth unspoken, yearning for a forum to speak. What has begun as a conversation with self: one that has enabled you to reconnect to the person who hid buried beneath your individual compromise with the world beckons to continue outward. This conversation and discovery of self that has begun with you, is waiting to meet the world. When we are all authentic to ourselves, we can only want others to follow the same principle for life. Beneath these social masks: there will be a time where can all share a unified language and have pride in our individual gaze of the world.

Share your Letters

It is empowering looking into a mirror and being able to see yourself for who you truly are. It is even more gratifying holding up your reflection of self to the world. This courageous act will enable yourself to completely free any inhibitions from the past, and share your optimism for the future.

Through your words, your Letters of Gratitude has the power impart a more colorful understanding of the world. The more people understand your interpretation of a word, the greater depth and breadth of the word. The more people that share, the better understanding we have of each other. Our mission is to unify each other by expanding the different views of the word.

If you wrote your letters with someone, undoubtedly they have a better understanding of your interpretation of the word, therefore a better understanding of you. We welcome your letters of gratitude. It gives us a greater understanding of people. Through the Letters of Gratitude, we aim to page by page: we weave our worlds. To bring people together so that we can share common languages while understanding we all see it differently. This will enable us to see people of free judgments and expectations and to encourage people to live the lives that they want for themselves.

If you wish to be a part of a future *Letters of Gratitude* publication, or a spotlight on our website, send us you Letters and/or you feedback on the process!
We will acknowledge all contributors (by name or anonymously).
thelettersofgratitude@gmail.com

Made in the USA
Lexington, KY
10 March 2014